THE
Archive Photographs
SERIES

LITTLEHAMPTON

Photographing the photographer, c. 1910. A photographer takes a snap of a man sitting astride the gunwale of the Littlehampton fishing boat *Risk*. Old Quay Wharf is in the background.

THE
Archive Photographs
SERIES

LITTLEHAMPTON

Compiled by
Ian Friel and Rebecca Fardell

CHALFORD

First published 1998
Copyright © Littlehampton Town Council, 1998

The Chalford Publishing Company
St Mary's Mill, Chalford,
Stroud, Gloucestershire, GL6 8NX

ISBN 0 7524 1123 3

Typesetting and origination by
The Chalford Publishing Company
Printed in Great Britain by
Bailey Print, Dursley, Gloucestershire

The circus comes to town, *c.* 1911. A circus procession - probably from Lord John Sanger's Circus - heading west along the High Street.

Contents

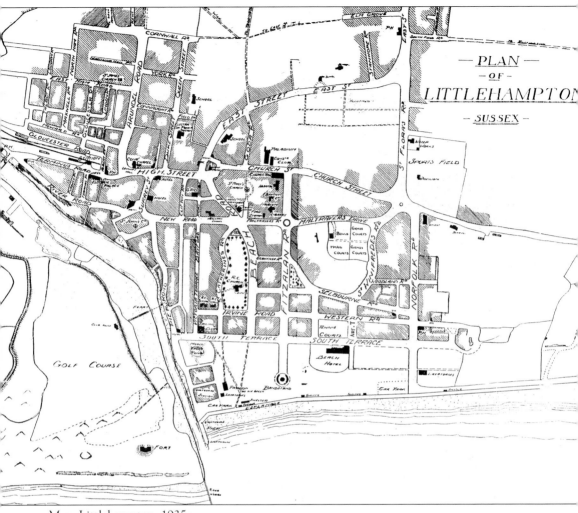

Map: Littlehampton, 1935.

View of Littlehampton from the top of St Mary's church tower, 1930s.

Introduction

This book is primarily about the social history of Littlehampton as revealed in old photographs. It is based entirely on the Littlehampton Museum photographic collection, which comprises the Arun District Council and Littlehampton Town Council collections. The museum now has over 7,400 prints, slides and negatives, ranging in date from the 1860s to the present, and the collection continues to grow. While significant parts of the collection have been purchased by the museum, or have been photographed by museum staff, it is probably true to say that the majority of the images are the result of generous public donations that began in the very earliest days of the museum in the late 1920s. This book, published in the museum's seventieth anniversary year, is dedicated with thanks to all those who have donated photographs to the museum, or who have allowed the museum to copy the precious historical images in their possession.

A Short History of Littlehampton

Littlehampton is a small coastal town with a population of around 24,000. It has a much longer history than many local people might imagine. The area was heavily settled in prehistoric and Roman times, and a tiny hamlet called 'Hampton' was already in existence by the time of the Domesday survey of 1086. The prefix 'Little' appears in the fifteenth century and is thought to have been coined by mariners to distinguish the small Sussex village from the great port of Southampton, then also called 'Hampton'.

Littlehampton grew slowly over the centuries and until the second half of the eighteenth century, when the first holiday visitors began to arrive, it was primarily a farming settlement. In the space of the next hundred years, the population rose tenfold, from 584 in 1801 to 5,954 in 1901, and the character of the town changed markedly. In 1801, Littlehampton consisted largely of flint and brick houses, clustered around the High Street and its connecting roads, with a scatter of buildings down by the beach. By 1901, the 'Beach' settlement had grown considerably, with late Georgian and Victorian terraces, and was physically linked with the old village centre, which had itself expanded. Littlehampton officially became a town in 1853, with the creation of its Local Board of Health, and by 1901 it was an Urban District, incorporating the outlying villages of Wick and Toddington.

Until the second half of the nineteenth century, seafaring and shipbuilding were major factors in the local economy. Littlehampton has never been a big port, but in the 1800s, Littlehampton ships and seafarers sailed all over the world and the harbour was visited regularly by ships carrying coal from north east England and by vessels with cargoes of timber from the Baltic. Between 1863 and 1882 the town even had a cross Channel ferry service linking it with Honfleur in France. The closure of the service and the decline of local shipbuilding in the 1880s had a serious effect on the fortunes of the port.

However, much of the town's growth between 1801 and 1914 was driven by the holiday trade. This was particularly true after the construction of the town centre railway terminus in 1863, which helped to open up Littlehampton to the mass market of working-class holidaymakers and day trippers from London and other large cities. Many of the town's nineteenth-century buildings were originally constructed as boarding accommodation for visitors. The real 'boom time' seems to have come between about 1890 and 1910: the numbers of boarding houses more than doubled in the 1890s (to over 200 by 1899) and by 1911 the population had crossed the 8,000 mark.

The twentieth century has seen the town grow larger, but at a rather slower rate. The population has increased fourfold in the last ninety years or so. New post-war estates were built around Wick, and on the eastern side of town the construction of the Beaumont Park estate led to the filling in of the strip of countryside that had hitherto separated Littlehampton and Rustington.

The town's economy has also become much more diverse. The holiday trade remained strong into the 1960s (Littlehampton station's peak year was 1957, with over 539,000 passengers), but competition from cheap foreign holidays began to take its toll on Littlehampton, as with so many other British resorts, and the numbers of staying visitors began to fall. That said, the town still attracts hundreds of thousands of day-trippers each year and recent developments, such as the revival of the summer regatta, have helped to bring many more people to the town.

Declining employment in the holiday trade has to some extent been offset by the development of light industry and commerce and The Body Shop cosmetics firm is now the largest local commercial employer. Boatbuilding, fishing and water sports have helped to keep the harbour alive, and since the 1960s the port has become much busier, both with pleasure craft and with ships delivering cargoes of marine aggregates and other construction materials.

In 1851, Littlehampton people could perhaps have said, with some justice, that theirs was a seafaring town, for maritime activity was one of the largest single employers. In 1901 and 1951, they could have said, with equal justice, that it was a holiday town. At the end of the twentieth century, it is much less easy to make statements of this kind and the future is unlikely to be just a repeat of the past. However, for the foreseeable future Littlehampton is likely to continue to be a seaport and a seaside resort and also - it is to be hoped - a town with a strong sense of its own identity.

One
Streetscapes
and Landscapes

Littlehampton High Street, 1863. This is the earliest known photograph of the High Street and shows a view looking westwards from the eastern end of the High Street. The 'Moore Grocer' sign was for the shop of James Richard Moore, a grocer and cheesemonger, who is known to have been in business in the town in the mid-1860s.

The High Street at the time of Queen Victoria's Golden Jubilee, 1887. This photograph was taken at the junction with Surrey Street and shows the Dolphin Hotel on the right. The people are, left to right: Miss Toy, Mr Toy (who both ran small private schools), George Groom (grocer), Mr Snewin (builder), Mr Thomas (blacksmith) and the boy is Teddy Pannell.

The western end of the High Street, *c.* 1960.

Cottages in Duke Street, probably late 1930s. This terrace was constructed in the 1840s as working-class accommodation by the Littlehampton builder Robert Bushby. They were demolished in 1953, although part of a similar row across the road survives as Ockenden's garden department.

Victoria Terrace, Bayford Road, probably 1920s. This terrace was built in the late 1870s and early 1880s, primarily as holiday accommodation. In 1910, forty-three of the fifty-five houses were boarding houses. Victoria Terrace is said to be the longest terrace of its kind in the country.

Surrey Street, early to mid-1860s. The Norfolk Hotel was one of the town's leading hostelries, and survived until after the Second World War. The shop bearing the Prince of Wales' feathers belonged to the tailor and draper William Dyer, a prominent, if controversial, local figure. Dyer's Cottages, next door to his shop, were destroyed by fire in 1868.

Surrey Street, c. 1960. The same view as the previous photograph, but nearly a century later. The Norfolk Hotel has gone and only one section of Dyer's shop still stands, with a Woolworths store (built in the 1930s) on the site of Dyer's Cottages. Hare's Garage can be seen on the left.

River Road, early 1920s. The Ship and Anchor was one of six pubs once to be found in River Road, presumably catering for a large and regular seafaring clientele! The large house behind the telegraph pole was once the home of Joseph Robinson, Victorian Littlehampton's wealthiest ship owner.

A new terrace in East Ham Road, early 1900s. The construction of East Ham Road began in the early 1890s, but by 1898 it contained only eight buildings. However, over seventy houses had been added by 1910, with a new church (St James's) on the corner. The photograph shows a group of builders and decorators, perhaps employees of Bicknell & Stone, the company that built much of the street.

Wick Street, looking south, *c.* 1936. The settlement of Wick was in existence by the late thirteenth century. It grew up along Wick Street, as a separate village from Littlehampton. Wick was in Lyminster parish until 1901, when it became part of Littlehampton Urban District.

Lyminster Road, looking north, early 1900s. The Globe Inn was opened in about 1869 and much of the Norway Cottages terrace was built in the 1870s. The buildings still stand, although their surroundings have been totally transformed, with a large roundabout in the foreground and one of The Body Shop buildings on the left.

Fields at Court Wick Farm, 1952. Littlehampton was still being called a village in the 1850s and even now retains some farmland within its boundaries. Signs of Littlehampton's rural past can still be seen in different parts of the town.

Toddington, early 1900s. Toddington, like Wick, was a small hamlet of medieval origin. This photograph shows Toddington farmhouse, a building of late sixteenth- or early seventeenth-century date, and one of the oldest houses in the Littlehampton area. Toddington was incorporated into Littlehampton Urban District in 1901 and over the past century the spread of urban building has gradually merged it physically with the town.

Looking south down Church Street, c. 1913. This shows the Olympic Hall in the distance and the junction with Fitzalan Road on the left. The Olympic Hall was opened in 1910 as a roller skating rink, but later became the Palladium Cinema. The site is now occupied by the Amenic Court flats ('Amenic' is 'cinema' backwards!).

The junction of East Street and St Flora's Road, 1927. St Flora's Road was laid out at the end of the nineteenth century and the houses seen here are some of the middle-class 'villas' that were built on the east side of the road. The house on the left with the flat gable end is 'Green Bushes', the home of Mary Neal (d. 1944), a nationally important figure in the revival of English folk dance and song at the turn of the century.

Beach Road, early 1900s. Beach Road was not really built up until the latter part of the nineteenth century. The building on the right was constructed in 1893 as the town offices, the first purpose-built local government office in the town, and is used today by Spofforths.

Norfolk Road, early 1900s. The southern end of Norfolk Road existed from around 1800. The New Inn, on the left in this photograph, was built in around 1802. Norfolk Road, South Terrace and the surrounding roads became part of what was called 'The Beach' or 'Beach Town', a Georgian and Victorian development comprising houses, shops and holiday accommodation, some distance from the old centre of Littlehampton.

Surrey House (right) and Surrey Cottage, mid to late nineteenth century. Surrey House was originally named Berkeley House, and was constructed in 1790 by the Earl of Berkeley for his mistress (or, as an 1830s guide delicately put it, 'for his Countess before her title was recognized'). It was later bought by the Earl of Surrey, and subsequently became a boys' boarding school. It was demolished in 1948.

Engraving of Western Road, 1861. Built in the late 1850s, these houses were probably intended as holiday accommodation.

South Terrace, probably *c.* 1870-90. Much of South Terrace was developed as holiday accommodation for the well-off visitors who started coming to Littlehampton from the later eighteenth century onwards. With Georgian terraces at the eastern end and late Victorian terraces at the other, South Terrace demonstrates, to some extent, the development of the English seaside terrace in the nineteenth century.

Sea Road, looking from Rustington towards Littlehampton, probably early 1900s. This photograph shows how rural the coastline between Littlehampton and Rustington was. The gateway visible in the middle ground of the picture is the entrance for Rustington Convalescent Home which was built in 1897.

A mechanical digger at work, Mewsbrook, mid-1930s. Mewsbrook was a mosquito-infested swamp in the countryside between Littlehampton and Rustington, not far from Rustington Convalescent Home. Discussions about turning the land into a small park and boating lake began in 1935 and Littlehampton Urban District Council eventually bought Mewsbrook by means of a compulsory purchase order.

A landscape transformed: Mewsbrook, probably 1939. The Mewsbrook Pleasure Grounds opened to the public in 1939.

Two

Growing Up

Arthur and Eva Robinson with their son Arthur Rupert in the garden of 'Ennerdale', River Road, c. 1916. Captain Robinson, a member of the Littlehampton ship owning family, built 'Ennerdale' in 1912. When he retired, he did a great deal of carving and erected a summerhouse from unused ship timbers. Eva Robinson was the daughter of Ealing Pitt, an owner of the Beach Hotel.

The Duke of Norfolk at the opening of the Swing Bridge, 27 May 1908. The Duke's children and those of the Littlehampton townsfolk would have had very different upbringings and meetings such as this must have caused some mutual embarrassment.

Children in a studio portrait by A. King, 1900s. These children have been photographed with a seaside backdrop and props. This theme accounts for the informal striped jumpers of the two older boys. The picture is in the form of a cabinet card. Such cards were very popular, especially when photograph albums became common in the late nineteenth century.

Children playing off the pier on East Beach, *c.* 1910. Littlehampton was known as 'The Children's Paradise' at the turn of the century.

Children playing in the snow on East Beach, January/February 1963. The winter of 1962/63 was the coldest since 1740, and nearly fifty people died. From late December 1962 until March 1963, much of Sussex was under deep snow and the River Arun froze in several places. It could, however, be fun if you were a child!

Wick School children in *c.* 1904-5. Wick School (now Lyminster County Infants), was erected in 1878 at a cost of £2,500 and intended for 330 children. It was one of the many Board Schools that were built as a result of the 1870 Education Act, which saw the state taking some responsibility for education for the first time.

Children from Wick School ready to leave for the opening of the Swing Bridge, 27 May 1908. The opening of the Swing Bridge was a day of great celebrations in Littlehampton. There was a grand tea party on Rope Walk for all the town's schoolchildren, followed by sports.

Children in the playground of East Street School, probably early 1900s. This unusual photograph was taken before Goda Road was built (1908). East Street School is now The Flintstone Centre.

Girls in their classroom at East Street School, c. 1920. East Street School opened in 1878 and was the Board School for girls and infants; the boys were based in Church Street. In 1939, the girls moved to Elm Grove School.

Pellew House School. Pellew House, Norfolk Road, was opened as a school by Mrs Arnett Braithwaite in 1907. Littlehampton had a large number of private schools of varying standards; indeed a total of forty-one such schools existed at one time or another in Victorian Little-hampton. There was a particular boom in the 1890s when thirteen institutions were established, a fact which may reflect the growing prosperity and population of the town towards the end of the nineteenth century.

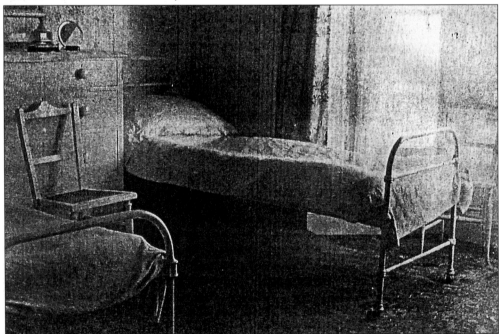

Dormitory in Pellew House School. These were extremely spartan compared to the public rooms.

Drawing room in Pellew House. It is unclear whether this was for use by staff or pupils.

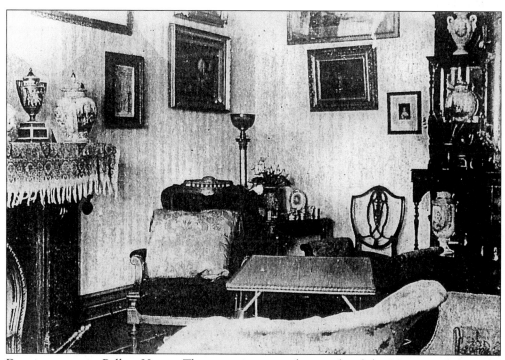

Drawing room in Pellew House. The room is a typical example of the Victorian fashion for clutter in rooms.

A classroom at Groombridge House School, probably 1920s. This picture is a poor advertisement for the school. The paint is peeling off the walls, the desks are covered with graffiti and the blackboard is in need of a new coat of paint.

Part of a photograph showing the children and staff of Groombridge House School, December 1921. Pellew House became Groombridge School when the Misses Langfield moved their educational establishment there from South Terrace. Private schools often changed their names and locations as they were the personal business of those who ran them. Unlike Pellew House, Groombridge was coeducational.

The gymnasium at Rosemead School, probably *c*. 1920. Rosemead began as a boys' preparatory school in 1907, specializing in preparing boys for the Royal Navy. It was founded as a girls' school in 1919 by Miss Nita Sharpe and Miss Ruth Young, the boys moving to nearby Dorset House School. In 1995 it merged with Lavant School and moved to Chichester.

Bride and groom leaving St Mary's church, Littlehampton, *c*. 1910. Note the carpet that has been laid out for the bride and groom to walk down.

A Victorian family, 1894. These photographs were presented to Mr and Mrs W.H. Weller on 13 November 1894. William Holloway Weller was based in Surrey Street and worked as postmaster from the 1860s to 1895; he combined this with his watchmaking business. There has been a photograph attached to the lower family group; perhaps this man was unable to be present when the picture was taken.

Three
Work and Workplaces

Household servants, c. 1907. The photograph appears to show a housekeeper flanked by two parlour maids. Being 'in service' was one of the most common paid occupations for women at this time. The photograph is on a postcard sent by 'Gerty' to a Mrs Hayes, living in Western Court, Littlehampton. It bears the following enigmatic message: 'When the Mrs is away the Mice will play'.

Banfield's shop, between *c.* 1878 and 1889. 'Timmy' Banfield began as a market gardener in Ferry Road, but by 1878 he had opened a greengrocery in the High Street. The shop was demolished in 1889 when Clifton Road was cut through to join the High Street. From the photograph and other sources, it is clear that Banfield did not just sell vegetables. The following quotation is taken from *Reminiscences of Littlehampton* by Eva Robinson and J.S. Heward (1933): '....."Timmy" Banfield's shop, where Mrs Littlehampton bought her rabbits, fowls and snipe, or if her pocket was not a deep one, she could buy five sparrows for one penny, or half a dozen thrushes, or as many blackbirds for a pie. For in Banfield's shop the little songsters could be seen, spitted on wooden sticks - dainty morsels for the unimaginative'.

Boniface's fishmonger's, 4 Selborne Road, *c.* 1900. This shop was in business between around 1895 and 1911. The building, with its attractive curved first-floor windows, still stands.

Milkmen outside the Victoria Dairy, Western Road, *c.* 1910. The Victoria Dairy was in business from the early 1900s to the mid-1930s. In 1910 it was one of eleven dairies in the town. The photograph shows two methods of delivering milk - the traditional one using a churn carted round the streets and the more modern one using milk bottles. Milk bottles did not become common until the 1920s.

White & Müller's shop, Beach Road, *c.* 1900. White & Müller's business began in Norfolk Road in the early 1890s, but by 1899 they had moved to this shop in Beach Road. They remained in business until the eve of the First World War, but the firm then disappeared. It is possible that Müller, with his Germanic name, was interned as an enemy alien.

George Groom's Pier Road shop, *c.* 1900-07. George Groom was a grocer, china dealer and wine merchant, trades that benefited from the rapid growth of the town between 1890 and 1910. By 1905 Groom had four shops, in the High Street, Western Road, Pier Road and Wick Street. He became Chairman of the Urban District Council, and at one time lived in the Manor House.

'Ockenden's supply anything' carnival float, Maltravers Drive, 1920s. Ockenden's is the oldest firm in Littlehampton, founded in 1802, and has been in the ironmongery business for most of that time. This float, bedecked with fairies, was advertising 'Fairy Dyes'.

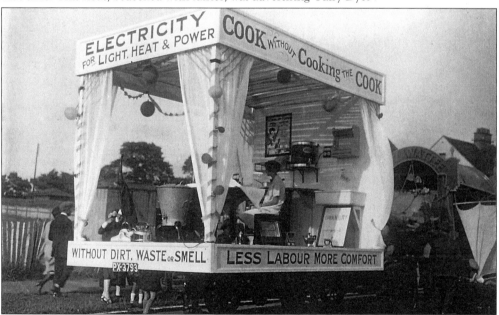

Littlehampton carnival float, late 1920s. The Sussex Electricity Supply Company built the town's first electricity generating station in Duke Street in 1922. The float displays a host of modern electrical appliances but it is doubtful if many onlookers could have afforded them. Even in the late 1930s, the two most common electrical appliances in British households were the radio and the electric iron: the great boom in electrical consumer goods did not come until the 1950s.

Wallpaper display, Sole's shop, 1960. D.S. Sole Ltd were decorators' merchants at 32 Beach Road.

Lloyd's Bank under construction, c.1903. Originally built for the Capital and Counties Bank Ltd, this was the second permanent bank building in the town - the first was the striking 1897 London & County Bank in the High Street (now NatWest). The construction of new banks at the turn of the century was a sign of the town's growing prosperity: in 1890 there had only been two part-time sub-branches in Littlehampton.

Cycle repair shop at Clark & Robinson's, High Street, *c.* 1900. Clark & Robinson were in business between the mid-1890s and the eve of the First World War. They were general ironmongers and engineers and also undertook the repair and construction of bicycles. The bench drill and vice shown in the photograph are now in the Littlehampton Museum collection.

Butler's carriage workshop, High Street, *c.* 1910. Alfred Butler started his carriage-building firm in around 1908. The mainstay of a workshop like this was probably the maintenance and repair of horse-drawn vehicles, although some automobile and cycle work was undertaken. Butler later seems to have gone into the motor coach business.

Staff at the Littlehampton Motor Company, May 1920. Probably once the largest car firm in the town, the Littlehampton Motor Company was in existence between around 1914 and the late 1920s. In 1920, the company had its works and offices in River Road, and a garage in Surrey Street; this was later used by Hare's.

Seed cleaning plant, Court Wick Farm, 1946. This machinery was used to dress seed to help protect it against disease and wireworm. Vinnicombe and Son farmed at Court Wick for many years and operated as seed merchants.

Frontage of Constable's Anchor Brewery, probably early 1900s. The Constable family took over the brewery in the High Street in the late 1850s or early 1860s, and converted it to steam power in 1871 with the addition of a steam engine and a large chimney. The company produced mineral waters as well as beer, and also ran the Swallow Brewery in Arundel. Beer brewing continued at Littlehampton until 1917 and in 1921, Constable's amalgamated with Henty's of Chichester. Much of the old Anchor Brewery was pulled down in the 1970s. All that remains is the old brewery shop, now Threshers off-licence, and the road name 'Anchor Springs'.

Water pumping equipment at Duke & Ockenden's workshop, Ferry Wharf, c. 1890. Founded in 1887, on the basis of an earlier company started by the Ockendens, Duke & Ockenden's primary business lay in the construction of water supply equipment. Later known by the acronym DANDO (for D and O), the company became one of the leaders in its field and Dando Drilling International is still very active in the business.

DANDO engineers making test borings for the new Littlehampton swing bridge, 1907. In the same year, DANDO was involved in a major project to restore the foundations of St Paul's Cathedral in London.

Mechanized timber wagon, Butt's timber yard, probably early 1900s. This wagon was devised by one of the firm's staff. John Eede Butt & Sons were timber merchants and builders, founded in around 1828. The firm imported timber from Scandinavia, the Baltic and Russia, and slate from North Wales, and became a major local supplier of building materials. Butt's were taken over by Travis Arnold in 1944 and their yard is now used by Travis Perkins.

Butt's first motor vehicle, early 1900s. As a company, Butt's appears to have had something of an interest in innovation: in 1879, for example, they acquired two of the first telephones in Britain, to link the firm's Littlehampton and Brighton offices. For this reason, Butt's had the phone number 'Littlehampton No. 1'.

Steeplejacks at work, Butt's timber yard, c. 1933. The chimney belonged to Butt's steam sawmill.

Connaught Road School staff, 2 November 1938. Connaught School opened as a boys' school in 1900. Although it later became a mixed primary school, it was still a single-sex establishment when this photograph was taken. The teachers shown are, left to right: back row Mr J. Webster, Mr W. Edmunds, Mr Blunden, Mr D. Chubb, Mr J.H. Bentley; front row Mr C.J. Etherington, Miss D. Chandler, Mr W.J. Norris, unknown, and Mr J. Macleod.

Four
The Holiday Trade

Holidaymakers on the East Beach, early 1900s. The large sandcastle shows that the sand close by the promenade was quite deep at this date. From the turn of the century until at least the 1930s, Littlehampton was proudly promoted as 'The Children's Paradise'.

The Hewitt sisters of Littlehampton on the beach, *c.* 1910. The bathing machines in the background were once a common sight at most British seaside resorts. Designed to be rolled into the sea, they were intended to make it possible to segregate the sexes when they were bathing. Victorian Littlehampton had obsessively detailed byelaws against 'indecent' mixed bathing but these seem to have been largely ignored by the early 1900s.

In the sea, East Beach, Littlehampton, 1928.

Littlehampton swimming pool, East Beach, 1933. This was a concrete enclosure designed to fill with seawater at high tide. It stood off Norfolk Road between 1929 and 1934 but was demolished when the lease expired. The town did not have a fixed swimming pool again until Littlehampton Swimming Centre opened in the 1980s.

Car park by the Pier, 1930s. Although motor cars were still the preserve of the middle and upper classes in the inter-war years, the numbers of car owners grew considerably. 'Weekending' by car became increasingly popular, to the benefit of places like Littlehampton.

Café and chalets on the West Beach, 1930s. Nowadays the West Beach and the dunes are part of a Site of Special Scientific Interest with scarcely any buildings. Things were very different in the 1930s. Two local companies developed beach huts or 'sand chalets' and cafés on the West Beach. One of them boasted a 'VITA-GLASS Cafe… [for] coffee and cigarettes after your dip, where you can get a healthy sunburn in all weathers in safety and comfort'. The West Beach enterprises seem to have failed, although there was some limited development on the West Beach after the Second World War.

The Promenade and Green, *c.* 1914. The promenade was first laid out in the 1860s and with the Green forms one of the seafront's most distinctive features. The Green was left largely clear of major building on the instructions of the landowner, the Duke of Norfolk.

The bandstand on the Green, probably 1920s. The bandstand was used for many years for weekend concerts. Although it is long gone, the Green remains a popular spot for local people and visitors.

The old Beach Hotel, 1863. This is one of the earliest dated photographs of Littlehampton, and shows the original Beach Hotel on the Green. Constructed in the 1770s, it was the first purpose-built holiday hotel in Littlehampton. Visitors began to come to Littlehampton in the late 1760s, as sea bathing became more popular, and this Hotel was a modest attempt to offer them accommodation.

The new Beach Hotel, *c.* 1897-1905. The Beach Hotel was Littlehampton's premier holiday hotel for over ninety years. It replaced the old hotel and opened in around 1890. The hotel offered 'Every Comfort to Visitors', and in the early 1900s even had electric light. In the post-war years it attracted many wealthy and famous people but it eventually closed in the late 1980s and was demolished in 1994.

Camping at Rope Walk, 1930s. Camping became a popular form of recreation in the 1920s and 1930s, giving many people the opportunity of a cheap holiday, besides the health benefits that were believed to be associated with the activity.

Children playing by the Oyster Pond, early 1900s. The Oyster Pond was a storage basin for oysters, in use from at least the 1820s until about 1860. In the mid-1890s it became a storm-water reservoir, but was also rebuilt as an ornamental lake. For many decades it served as a model yacht pond and featured in various town regattas.

A goat cart on the Green, 1905. The two children and their lapdogs are attended by a nursery nurse, and may well have come from one of the better-off families holidaying in South Terrace or elsewhere in the 'Beach' area. Until the latter part of the nineteenth century, middle and upper-class visitors were the mainstay of Littlehampton's holiday trade and the town had a 'social season'.

Donkey rides near Butlin's Amusement Park, *c.* 1938. The donkey rides on Littlehampton beach were run for many decades by the Merrett family of Wick. The structure in the background is the base of Butlin's roller coaster, which bore more than a passing resemblance to the Roman Colosseum.

'Uncle Charlie' was Charles Speller, a theatrical performer who settled in Littlehampton. In the 1920s he managed the Casino theatre, on what is now the Harbour Park site, producing a variety of entertainments, but to visiting children he was probably best known for his Punch and Judy show.

'Uncle Terry' on the seafront, early 1930s. Harry Page (in the flat cap), otherwise known as 'Uncle Terry', ran stalls on the seafront during the 1930s. The other man in the photograph is Ernie Farrow.

'Uncle Terry's' stall on The Green, early 1930s. Harry Page did not just sell publications and sweets, but also ran a quiz, with prizes. Uncle Terry is the one dressed in the pierrot costume with 'ANSWERS' on the back.

'Uncle George's Children's Corner', on the Green, 1930s. Another of the local puppet shows.

'Hurrah! It's Butlin's', 1933. Billy Butlin opened his new amusement park at Littlehampton in 1933, on the site of the old Arun Mill and the Coastguard Cottages. Incorporating a massive blue-painted roller coaster, it represented 1930s seaside entertainment at its most uncompromising. Some local people objected strongly to it (the then museum curator described it as a 'Whooppee City') but it helped to revive Littlehampton's fortunes as a seaside resort. The site is now Harbour Park.

Water dodgems at Butlin's Amusement Park, *c.* 1933. Combining people, water and electricity in this fashion may not now appear particularly safe, but as far as is known, this novel dodgem pool did not cause any serious injuries!

Landing for the *Nancy Lee*, 1920s. The *Nancy Lee* was one of a number of motorboats that plied the river in the inter-war years. The *Nancy Lee* later took part in the 1940 Dunkirk evacuation.

A trip on the Arun, August 1926. River trips have been a part of the holiday scene at Littlehampton since the nineteenth century. The motorboat is probably one of the two *Britannias*, built in the early 1920s. This postcard photograph was one of a number taken on the same day, each timed and dated precisely because the photographer wished to sell them to the trippers as souvenirs.

Five

Public Services and Public Life

Littlehampton Post Office staff, 1922. Littlehampton's first post office was in Surrey Street. It moved to the new High Street Arcade in 1922, at first occupying the premises that are now used by Belchamber & Company.

East Preston Union Workhouse. Constructed by the Littlehampton builder Robert Bushby, this workhouse was opened in 1871. It was intended for the poor, sick and old who lived between Broadwater and Climping. Conditions were harsh, so that all but the very needy would be deterred from claiming poor relief. Workhouses were finally abolished in the 1920s and the Workhouse eventually became an old people's home.

Water Tower in St Flora's Road, c. 1906. Building of the 91 ft high water tower began in 1880 and it was in use from 1882 until 1952. The tower was finally demolished in 1961 and Parkside Evangelical church now stands on the site. The event in the foreground is probably Hadleigh House School sports day, which was held on the sports field. Note the policeman who appears to be guarding cups.

Workmen laying a 10 inch water main in Wick Street, 1898. Although Littlehampton had mains water in 1882, it was some time before it was extended to the residents of Wick. Whilst there was agreement that the water in Wick was unhealthy and unsanitary, there was much debate about who was responsible for providing piped water and who should bear the costs. Water pipes were finally laid in 1898 by the local firm of Duke and Ockenden.

The town pump in Church Street just before it was dismantled, 1933. The pump stood outside the Manor House and a plaque now commemorates the site.

Two men outside the offices of the West Sussex Gazette in Beach Road, *c.* 1910. 'Randalls' can be see reflected in the windows: this was a milliner's shop which was in Beach Road until around 1911. Identifying this photograph was difficult but the 'Randalls' reflection provided a vital clue as to where it was taken.

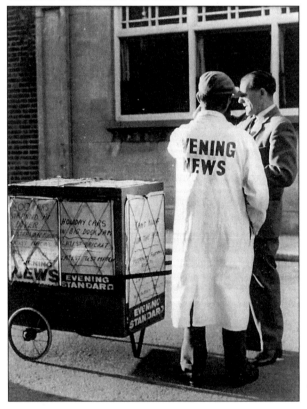

Newspaper seller in Arcade Road, 1966. The windows in the background of this photograph are those of the present Post Office.

Wick Post Office, Wick Street, c. 1900. Wick Post Office was at a number of sites before it reached its present location. George Taulbut was a bootmaker who lived just south of Wick Hall. He took over the Post Office at the turn of the century and moved it into his premises.

Sorting room of the new Post Office in the Arcade, 1922. Following the introduction of the penny post in 1840, the postal service grew rapidly. One result of this was the need for places to have more precise addresses, though most Littlehampton houses did not begin to acquire numbers until the mid-1870s.

Littlehampton Fire Brigade, mid-1890s. A volunteer fire brigade had been established in Littlehampton in 1874; it was only from 1938 that local authorities had to provide an efficient fire service, free of charge, for its citizens.

Aftermath of a fire in Western Road, *c.* 1895. The debris from the fire can be clearly seen at the side of the road. The archway on the right of the picture is the entrance to stables that later housed Harris' Riding School.

Fire in Littlehampton High Street, 7 June 1933. This fire engine appears to be the more modern of the two appliances that Littlehampton possessed in the 1930s.

Firewomen Ross, Vickes, Hollis, Standing, Temlett and Bodd with Fire Officer Cole outside Littlehampton Fire Station during the Second World War. When the National Fire Service was formed in 1941, it was necessary to take on women for watchroom duties, as drivers, cooks and for administrative work.

The first Littlehampton lifeboat in the Jubilee Parade in Terminus Road, 1887. The RNLI established a lifeboat station at Littlehampton in 1884. The town's first lifeboat was *Undaunted*, which can be seen taking part in the parade. Manned by a combination of coastguards and local fishermen, *Undaunted* had been transferred from Chichester Harbour when the lifeboat station there was closed.

Crew of the *Brothers Freeman* lifeboat making a presentation to one of their number. *Brothers Freeman* was provided out of a legacy to the RNLI by Mr Francis H. Freeman and was in service from 1904 until 1921. In this photograph, some of the crew are wearing their cork lifejackets.

Brothers Freeman being launched at Fisherman's Quay. *Brothers Freeman* was a self-righting, ten-oar rowing boat, and cost £800. During her seventeen years of service she saved ten lives. When she had finished at Littlehampton, she saw four more years' service at Plymouth.

Littlehampton's first motor ambulance, *c.* 1919. This First World War vehicle replaced the St John's Ambulance Brigade's Ashford Litter (a 'walking ambulance', or stretcher on wheels). It is said that the motor ambulance was prone to excessive bouncing unless weighted down by a concrete block! The Brigade acquired a new Austin ambulance in 1934.

First Aid Hut, 1930s. Since 1908, the Littlehampton St John's Ambulance Brigade volunteers have provided first aid for residents and visitors alike.

St John's Ambulance children's float, Beach Road, 1932. Until local authorities became responsible for providing an ambulance service, the task was undertaken by St John's Ambulance volunteers. The float seems to be part of a fundraising event; none of those taking part appear to be enjoying themselves.

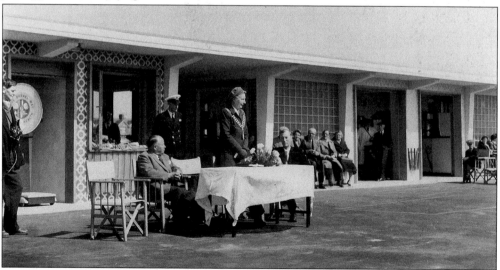

Flora McDonald speaking at the opening of the permanent kiosks at the western end of the Promenade in April 1957. Flora McDonald had become the first female chairman of Littlehampton Urban District Council the previous year.

Littlehampton Urban District Council, April 1938. This photograph was taken in the grounds of the Manor House which became the Council Offices in 1933. The grassed area is now part of the car park. Littlehampton Urban District Council was responsible for local government in the town from 1895 until the establishment of Arun District Council in 1974.

Six
Travel and Transport

Littlehampton swing bridge soon after its construction in 1908. The bridge was opened by means of a small engine, allowing ships to pass. It was in service for many years but by the 1960s the bridge was becoming increasingly unsuited to modern traffic. The swing bridge was dismantled in 1981 but the modern footbridge is in the same position and stands on the swing bridge's enormous piers.

Littlehampton chain ferry after an accidental stranding on the west bank, 1904. The chain ferry service opened in 1825. It consisted of a simple pontoon, pulled across the river by means of a chain, operated by two men. The original wooden ferry was replaced by a steel-hulled version in the early 1870s and this remained in service until the opening of the adjacent swing bridge in 1908.

Two motor cars on the chain ferry, c. 1906.

The chain ferry leaving Littlehampton, 1908. The chain ferry, or "ferry barge" was taken to the river Hamble near Southampton, for conversion into a houseboat. The Revd Green, vicar of Climping, was one of many proponents of the new swing bridge who were delighted to see the back of the old vessel.

POST CARD

THIS SPACE, AS WELL AS THE BACK, **MAY NOW BE USED FOR COMMUNICATION,** BUT FOR INLAND ONLY

HF ADDRESS ONLY
TO BE WRITTEN HERE

W. E. COLLINGS,
17, HIGH STREET,
LITTLEHAMPTON.

FAREWELL TO THE FERRY BARGE.

And so the old ramshackle pontoon is gone!
Hurrah! for good riddance, and victory won!
Did she take all her lovers to sea with her too?
If not, when they miss her, O, what will they do?

Will they weep and lament as they sit on the shore?
Or be off to Southampton to see her once more?
God bless them! I say, for we pity them now:
O, how could they love such a dirty old dhow?

Pre-historic was she? Was she built ere the Ark?
Then surely 'twas time she were burnt in the dark:
When fireworks were going why *did* they spare that?
O, why not have burnt her with Kilkenny Cat?

1908.   H. GREEN, Vicar, Clymping.

Workmen on the swing bridge, 1908.

The Golf Ferry, late 1920s or early 1930s. Littlehampton has had a small boat ferry since at least the seventeenth century. In the first half of this century it was often called the 'Golf Ferry', because it was used to carry golfers to and from the Littlehampton Golf Course on the west bank.

Lyminster level crossing, between 1907 and 1914. The railway first came to the Littlehampton area in 1846, but the original London, Brighton and South Coast Railway station (close by this crossing) was 1½ miles north of the town and very inconvenient. The station closed in 1863 when the main Littlehampton terminus opened but it was briefly reopened between 1907 and 1914 as a 'rail motor halt'.

Littlehampton station, 1900. This view shows part of the goods shed and goods yard of the 1863 station. The goods shed still exists, but the main station was pulled down in 1938, to be replaced by a 'temporary' structure that stood until 1988! The holiday trade meant that Littlehampton was a busy terminus, reaching its peak in 1957, when over 539,000 passengers passed through the station.

Littlehampton station staff, early 1900s. Edward Tanner, seen here surrounded by his staff, was stationmaster between the 1890s and the 1920s. The three boys in the small peaked hats worked on W.H. Smith's station bookstall.

Railway accident at Littlehampton station, 4 August 1920. Rail crashes have been relatively rare at Littlehampton, but this accident became internationally known. Due to human error, the air brakes failed to work as the train was coming into the station, and it ploughed through the buffers and the station wall, ending up halfway across Albert Road. Thirteen people were injured but fortunately there were no deaths.

Railway staff at Littlehampton, 1936. The atmosphere in this shot of Southern Railway staff is a world away from the stiff formality of the earlier staff photograph. The London, Brighton and South Coast Railway was amalgamated with other companies in 1923 to form the Southern Railway.

Harris' horse bus outside Littlehampton station, 1920s. From the 1840s onwards, horse buses linked Littlehampton's railway stations with other parts of town. Harris' were in the business from around 1890 to around 1930, but eventually the horse buses gave way to taxis and motor buses.

Dr Last's horse and trap, March 1908. Dr Last worked in Littlehampton between 1902 and 1938. This trap was used for his rounds in the early years of the practice and was driven by his coachman, Mr Gander (shown in the photograph). It was replaced by a motor car before the First World War and Mr Gander became the Last's gardener.

Horse-drawn timber wagon, New Road, probably 1920s or 1930s. Horse-drawn transport survived longer in some areas of work than in others, as in some cases it was cheaper to use horses. The timber shown here probably came from Butt's timber yard, to the right of the photograph.

Lady Mary, a Commer charabanc belonging to Norris and Co. of Littlehampton, *c.* 1913. Littlehampton's first motor bus service opened in about 1907, when a Worthing to Arundel route was started. Charles Norris and Co. were motor engineers and bus proprietors in Pier Road and ran a small fleet of charabancs, but the company was short lived.

Randall's removals lorry, probably 1920s. The lorry in this photograph was probably a military surplus vehicle from the First World War. Many small firms sprang up in the 1920s using cheap, ex-military transport and a similar phenomenon occurred after the Second World War. Randall's company started in about 1925.

An excursion coach carrying the local St John's Ambulance Brigade, just before departing for Eastbourne in 1932. The coach has a removable roof.

An Austin Mini, Hare's Garage, Surrey Street, 1962. Hare and Sons' garage in Surrey Street opened in the 1930s, in premises which had been used by the former Littlehampton Motor Company.

Hare's Thatchway Garage, Wick, 1962.

Waiting for the swing bridge to close, Terminus Road, mid-1960s. When it opened in 1908, the swing bridge was regarded as a great new traffic artery for the town; by the 1960s, it was seen as an obstacle. Opening the bridge to allow ships to pass led to traffic queues, particularly on bank holidays, and the situation was made worse by breakdowns of the ageing bridge motor. The new A259 road bridge opened in 1973.

Seven
The River and the Sea

The crew of the brig *Ebenezer*, Lowestoft, 9 June 1908. The man wearing the trilby hat is Louis Robinson, the ship's master, and one of the sons of the owner, Joseph Robinson. The *Ebenezer* was a 177 ton collier brig, used mainly in the coal trade with the north east of England. Built at Shoreham in 1860, the *Ebenezer* was the last ship owned by Joseph Robinson: she was sold off during the First World War and in 1917 was sunk by a German U-Boat.

Eva Robinson christening a vessel at Harvey's shipyard, c. 1914. On Eva Robinson's left is her husband, Arthur Robinson (1870-1950), a member of the prominent local seafaring family. He was a ship designer and shipwright, and may well have designed the vessel being launched, which at this date would have been an auxiliary barge.

A sailing barge under construction at Harvey's yard, probably early twentieth century. The vessel is 'in frame' - in other words, the frames have been assembled but the planks have yet to be fastened on to the hull. This method was used for the construction of most wooden sea-going European vessels from the fifteenth century onwards.

The launch of the auxiliary barge *Wessex* at Harvey's yard, August 1918. The *Wessex* was an auxiliary barge, a sailing vessel with an auxiliary motor. The shipyard was established in 1837 and was bought by the Harvey family in the 1840s. They became significant builders of wooden sailing ships, but when the market for wooden merchantmen began to decline in the 1880s, they had to concentrate on the construction of sailing barges and on ship repair. The yard closed in 1921 and the site is now used by the boatbuilding yards of Osborne, Hillyard and Cunningham.

Two members of the Burtenshaw family in a pub, *c.* 1900. The two men on the right were members of the Burtenshaw family. The Burtenshaws came to Littlehampton in the early nineteenth century as fishermen and became well known figures in the life of the harbour. To judge from the photograph behind the bar, the pub is the Nelson and Victory, at the corner of Pier Road and South Terrace.

The fishing boat *Risk* of Littlehampton, *c.*1910. The boat's name may belie the common notion that seamen are superstitious! The *Risk* is shown tied up to Fisherman's Quay, just by Old Quay Wharf, close to the site of the modern RNLI station. Sail-driven fishing boats were still in use at Littlehampton in the 1930s.

The fishermen Harry Burtenshaw Snr and Harry Burtenshaw Jnr, probably 1930s. Harry Snr featured in *Lobsters*, a short film about lobster fishing made at Littlehampton in the mid-1930s by John Matthias and the internationally famous Hungarian artist Laszlo Moholy-Nagy.

The paddle tug *Jumna* leaving Littlehampton harbour, *c.* 1907. The *Jumna* worked in the harbour between the late 1880s and the First World War, towing ships in and out of the port, and even as far upriver as Arundel. A distinctive vessel, the *Jumna* featured on many postcards and the modern harbour master's launch is named after the tug.

The *Green Olive* of Littlehampton under sail, late nineteenth century. The *Green Olive* may have been a German-built ship. She was a 243 ton vessel registered at Littlehampton between 1883 and 1897.

The wreck of the *Constance Ellen* of Littlehampton at South Shields, November 1901. Forty Littlehampton ships were lost at sea between 1863 and 1904, half of them on the East Coast. Owned by Joseph Robinson and captained by his son Louis, the *Constance Ellen* was driven ashore at South Shields by a severe gale. Robinson and his crew were saved by the local Volunteer Life Brigade. He never forgot their courage, leaving the Brigade £3,500 in his will at his death in 1962.

Cargo steamer in Littlehampton harbour, c. 1910.

A sailing barge at Littlehampton, early twentieth century. Harvey's yard built this type of vessel.

Scandinavian merchant ships, Littlehampton, between 1908 and 1914. The ship nearest the camera was from Norway, and the two beyond it were Swedish. Most of the timber that came into the harbour at this date was imported by John Eede Butt and Sons: their main suppliers were in southern Norway and eastern Sweden. The last timber shipment came to Littlehampton in about 1988.

Sailing ships at Baltic Wharf, 1922. This photograph was taken in 1922, during the construction of new timber storage sheds for John Eede Butt and Sons. The ships are a four-masted schooner (left) and a barquentine and both had probably brought cargoes of timber from the Baltic.

Sailors at work on the bowsprit of the *Romanie*, Littlehampton, probably 1920s. Sailing ships continued to visit Littlehampton during the 1920s and 1930s. They were a picturesque sight but by this date most sea trade went in steamers or motor vessels. Ships like the *Romanie* represented a maritime world that was fast vanishing.

The *Stralsund* entering Littlehampton harbour, probably 1920s. The decks of the ship are piled high with a cargo of timber.

Unloading a timber ship at Littlehampton, probably 1920s. The ship appears to have come either from Russia or from the Baltic Republics.

The *Dagfrid*, a Swedish timber ship of the 1920s, at Baltic Wharf. Baltic Wharf took its name from the port's Baltic timber trade and was in use from at least the 1820s.

A steam collier unloading at the Railway Wharf, 1930s. Littlehampton participated in the coastal coal trade with the north east of England from at least the early nineteenth century but by the 1930s, the bulk of the imports at Littlehampton consisted of stone for the building industry. Seaborne coal imports finally ceased in the early 1950s.

The motorboat *Ma Joie II* under construction at Osborne's yard, Littlehampton, 1921. The boat was built for Captain Waring of the Waring and Gillow furniture firm. The workers include Horace Jupp, standing near the centre of the group, wearing a white boiler suit and cap. Originally a motor company, Osborne's have been in boatbuilding since 1920 and since the early 1950s have built every prototype RNLI lifeboat.

Aero engine powered boat on the Arun, 1930s. This boat was designed by Bill Trotman, a former RAF engineer. With two partners, he also set up a company in Rope Walk manufacturing outboard motors, called TSD (Trotman, Smith and Dow). Although the company is long gone, at least one TSD outboard was still being used regularly until the late 1980s!

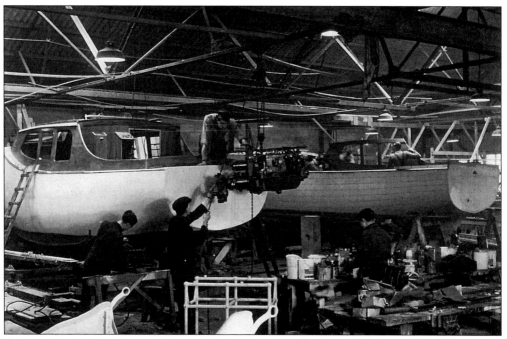

Cabin cruisers under construction at ARC Marine's works, River Road, *c.* 1950. ARC Marine was formed in Littlehampton during the Second World War and after the war undertook the construction of pleasure craft.

The frames of a wooden cabin cruiser at ARC Marine's works, River Road, *c.* 1950.

A dredger passing through Littlehampton swing bridge, April 1974. Littlehampton's import trade was very slow to revive after the Second World War. In the 1930s, annual imports had always exceeded 50,000 tons of cargo, but even the modest pre-war levels were not equalled until almost the mid-1960s. However, there was an enormous increase in the volume of imports in the late 1960s, with the introduction of large-scale offshore marine dredging of sand and gravel for the construction industry. This reached a peak in 1984 with the landing of 457,000 tons of these aggregates. Mid-1990s figures are lower, but still run at over 230,000 tons per year. Most of this work has been done by a small number of dredgers and their crews.

Eight

Leisure

Maurice Randall (right) shaking hands with Bernard, Duke of Norfolk, outside the Manor House during the presentation of a portrait of Gwendoline, Duchess of Norfolk, on 24 April 1936. Randall (1865-1950) was the son of a Littlehampton draper who became a professional seaman and went on to pursue a career as an artist.

Aerial view of excavations of the Bath House at Angmering Roman Villa, 1937. This massive excavation was sponsored by the playwright and Hollywood screenwriter R.C. Sherriff, who had a house in the area. The work was directed by Leslie Scott, a student of Mortimer Wheeler's, and involved both Littlehampton Museum and the Littlehampton Natural Science and Archaeology Society.

Littlehampton Natural Science and Archaeology Society excavations at Shepherd's Garden, Arundel Park, 1931. Founded in 1924 as the Nature and Archaeology Circle, the group became the LNSAS in 1931. This Iron Age and Roman site was one of a number investigated by the society.

94

Interior of Littlehampton Museum, probably late 1920s. The Littlehampton Natural Science and Archaeology Society played a central role in the foundation of Littlehampton Museum, which opened in 1928 in a specially built extension to the library (now the non-fiction section). The Museum moved to 12a River Road in 1965 and to its present home in the Manor House in 1991.

Saxon peasants: four members of the cast of the Littlehampton Episode of the Pageant of Arundel, August 1923. Staged at Arundel Castle, the pageant involved an enormous cast and took place over three days. Littlehampton's contribution to the Pageant was a re-enactment of the coming of Roger de Montgomery, the first earl, in 1070.

Harry Page (later also known as 'Uncle Terry') outside the Casino, probably 1920s. The revue advertised is *Paint & Powder*, a performance by 'Mrs 'Arris of the Sunday 'Erold'. Mrs 'Arris was one of the creations of Freddie Spencer, a popular performer, even with the landladies whom he pilloried. Harry Joseph also put on shows at the Casino during the winter months.

Street performance by Coastguard Cottages, 1904. This card was sent to Miss Ivy Stennell in Palmers Green, London, on 25 August 1904. Concert parties on the seafront were a common feature of holidays earlier this century. They would include songs, dances, short sketches, monologues, comedy and drama and were aimed at a family audience. Money would be collected at the end by taking round a hat.

Harry Joseph's troupe, *c.* 1911. Back row, left to right: Dan Lyall, Rex Kempton, Fred Preston, Gary Lynch. Front row, left to right: Floyd Gwyn, Kate Avey, Hector Strange, Mrs Joseph, Frank Hughes. Conductor: Harry Joseph. Harry Joseph formed his first pierrot troupe in Littlehampton in 1889. His performers won a national pierrot competition at the London Palladium in 1911 and in 1912 he opened a Kursaal, a combined pierrot and fun palace, which was demolished to make way for Butlins in the early 1930s.

Venus Competition, Tuesday 5 July 1955. The competition was won by Jean Tullett, who is in black on the right. Out of a possible 100 points, she scored 95 and won a £5 cash prize. Jean was a waitress at the Norfolk Sports Pavilion and it was her first beauty competition.

A brass ensemble, *c.* 1900.

Littlehampton Town Band, *c.* 1936. There has been music in Littlehampton since at least the late eighteenth century: the earliest known musical group was a church band at St Mary's Church in 1778.

Fair in Surrey Street, c. 1906. Littlehampton has had a May Fair for a very long time. From the late nineteenth century until the 1930s, gallopers were the major attraction at fairs and roundabout proprietors were at the top of the showland hierarchy. This photograph makes clear the difference between the boy from the fair and the one from the town.

Dancing at Surrey Street Fair, c. 1910. Littlehampton Fair was held in Surrey Street for many years; it was not always popular because it disrupted traffic and in 1933 it was moved to Linden Park. Dancing was an old feature of fairs and from the nineteenth century there were a number of rides, like the cakewalk and waltzer, which had a dancing movement.

Wick Carnival King and Queen, August 1946. Sheila Madron was crowned Carnival Queen, with Raymond Peskett as King.

The Littlehampton Launch Company's float for the 1957 carnival. The carnival has been a regular feature of town life since at least the early 1920s.

Participants in the Bonfire Society parade, 1904. Littlehampton's first Bonfire Society was disbanded in 1906. The present society was founded in 1952 with the aim of 'providing an evening of spectacular entertainment as a means of raising money for local good causes'. Whilst recent celebrations have explicitly avoided the anti-catholic overtones of Victorian events, Indian costume remains popular for Bonfire Society processions.

Cricket match, Arundel v. Littlehampton, 1889. This match ended in a draw. The earliest record of cricket in Littlehampton is of a game played on the Green between the Gentlemen of Sussex and Storrington Club, which took place on 2 July 1802.

Ladies' tennis match, probably early 1890s. This match was part of a tournament that took place on the Beach Hotel courts (the site is now occupied by Channel Keep). The contests on these courts were often of a high standard and attracted large crowds.

"THE BALLOON ASCENT"
LITTLEHAMPTON AUG 14. 1909

'The Balloon Ascent', Littlehampton, 14 August 1909. This was probably done by a stuntman who went up in a balloon and then parachuted back down to the ground. The man can be seen suspended from his parachute, with the balloon above him.

Littlehampton Cycle Club, 1899. The Cycle Club was founded in 1878 by Edmund Yorke who was a grocer in Western Road. To celebrate the inception of the club, three members went on a tour of the West Country, which was deemed a great success. The Cycle Club shared bank holiday sports meetings with the Athletic Club; these meetings were also the idea of Edmund Yorke and were very popular.

Firemen's Sports, c. 1906. Before local authorities took over responsibility for the fire brigade, raising money for it was the task of people in the town.

'A Mighty Kick', early 1900s. This football match took place on Littlehampton sports field and the photograph title is contemporary. Although there had been a number of different local sites for sport, the Duke of Norfolk donated this sports field to the town in 1897. The first football club to play on the sports field was the Swifts, which was established in 1893 but had to close down in around 1900 because so many of its players had left the town.

Littlehampton Football Club, late 1940s.

Wick Football Club, 1924-5. Wick Football Club was founded in 1891.

Golf links from a booklet of photographs, *Littlehampton, Sussex - The Gem of the South, c. 1922.* Littlehampton Golf Club was founded in 1889 on the west bank of the River Arun. It has seen some famous players, including Albert, Duke of York (later George VI), his brother the Prince of Wales and Field Marshal Earl Haig.

Maltravers Bowling Club, *c*. 1940. Third from left: Mrs Hewitt; fifth from left: Mr McCandish; sixth from left: Mrs Matthews; far right: Walter Whyman. Walter Whyman and his wife, Alice, moved to Littlehampton in 1935 and became active members of the Maltravers Bowling Club; Alice won many cups. They lived in Courtwick Road until Walter's death in 1946.

Whist drive, 1910 or 1911. This photograph was probably taken in the Olympic Hall, which opened in Church Street on 16 March 1910. It was said to be one of the best equipped skating rinks on the South Coast, but the fashion for skating was soon over and the Hall became a theatrical and then cinema venue. The Hall, long since known as the Palladium Cinema, was demolished in 1986. The last film to be shown was *E. T.*

Littlehampton Sailing and Motor Club dinghy race off Littlehampton, 1930s. The LSMC was founded in 1896, although a boating club did exist in the 1870s and there have been boating events at Littlehampton since at least the 1830s. Littlehampton now has two sailing clubs, the LSMC and the Arun Yacht Club, which was founded in 1956.

Sailing close to the wind, Littlehampton, 1930s. This dinghy can be seen in the previous photograph.

Man outside the Steam Packet Tavern, Terminus Road, *c.* 1910. This public house was named after the steam packet service which ran from Littlehampton to Honfleur, Normandy, from 1863 until 1882.

Nine

Gatherings and Gathering Places

Procession past Terminus Hotel during Queen Victoria's Jubilee celebrations in 1887. Ben Saigeman can be seen in the centre of the picture; he was the town crier and bell ringer. His family were bathing machine proprietors and Saigeman is said to have saved the lives of several people who got into difficulties whilst bathing.

The Duke of Norfolk and family at the opening of the Swing Bridge, 27 May 1908. This ceremony was performed by the Duke, attended by civic dignitaries from across the county. It attracted one of the biggest crowds in the town's history up to that time and was reported in the national press.

Funeral observances for Edward VII at Littlehampton, 1910. The smoke probably came from gunpowder set in recesses in the anvils, once a blacksmiths' tradition for marking public events.

Morris dancing on the Green, 27 July 1912. The precise event has yet to be identified. Morris dancing, although of ancient origins, was revived at the turn of the century by the pioneering work of the English Folk Dance and Song Society. One of the Society's major figures was Mary Neal, who later lived in Littlehampton.

Morris dancing on the Green, 27 July 1912.

Children's Special Service Mission on East Beach, August 1909. The Special Service Mission was run by Mr Lucas and his daughters. They would go along the beach and recruit children to join the meeting.

Children's Special Mission Service on East Beach, August 1909. A gentleman remembered the Mission's prayer meetings on the beach, and commented: 'There was Mr Lucas and his daughters, who were very attractive.... This chap Lucas was a terribly nice man....'

St Mary's Church Choir, *c.* 1900. This substantial choir sang at the parish church. The picture also includes the churchwardens who can be identified by their wands of office.

Members of St John's Church Choir, early 1900s. At the far right is Mr Cooper. St John's Church was a temporary wooden building in Pier Road, erected to house a breakaway group from St. Mary's Church in 1877. It was supported by voluntary offerings and closed in 1948. The temporary building was never replaced and was later used as a theatre.

The Church Lads' Brigade outside Wick Hall shortly before the Second World War. Wick Hall was built onto the front of a school in 1900; if you look at the Hall from Beaconsfield Road, you can still see the original school. The Hall was the headquarters of the Church Lads' Brigade. The bass drum in the picture was originally made for the 4th Battalion of the Royal Irish Regiment by a drum maker in Aldershot, probably in the late nineteenth century.

Annual supper of the women's section of the British Legion, March 1936. This picture was taken in the British Legion Hall, Maltravers Road, which was built in 1931 and is now the United Services Club.

Rally at the Constitutional Club, 1930s. The Constitutional Club is in Church Street, opposite Littlehampton Hospital.

A fête in the grounds of Littlehampton Hospital, Fitzalan Road, 1915. The purpose-built hospital in Fitzalan Road opened in 1911, replacing the adapted house in Surrey Street which had become the town's first hospital in 1904. This fund-raising fête had a nostalgic theme, hence the thatched cottages as stalls and the man in a smock. Although smocks had been common, they were no longer worn as protective clothing by agricultural labourers.

Procession down South Terrace during National Baby Week, 28 July 1926. Littlehampton acquired its first Infant Welfare Centre in 1915.

Opening of the new Council Offices at the Manor House, 21 March 1934. Littlehampton Urban District Council moved from offices in Beach Road to the Manor House. The new offices were opened by Joan Vera Strong and Eric George Laker, two locally born schoolchildren. Previously, the Manor House had been a private house. It is now home to Littlehampton Town Council and Littlehampton Museum.

Ten

War and Peace

A local soldier, c. 1900. The man in this portrait photograph by John White of Littlehampton may have been a territorial rather than a regular. Other photographs show him to have been a military bandsman, but to judge from the number of shooting trophies, he was also a crack shot.

A Royal Sussex Regiment band, late nineteenth century. The Royal Sussex Regiment band regularly performed at events in Littlehampton. During the First World War, the Royal Sussex probably had more enlistments from Littlehampton men than any other regiment: certainly 29 per cent of the town's war dead belonged to the county regiment.

Boys of the 2nd Littlehampton Boy Scout Troop, before the First World War. The 1st and 2nd Littlehampton Troops were formed before the First World War. Within nine months of the outbreak of the war, twenty-one Littlehampton boy scouts had enlisted. The 2nd Troop was not re-formed after the war. According to local scout groups, its title was kept as a memorial to those scouts who had been killed.

Ammunition steamers in Littlehampton Harbour, about 16 January 1918. Littlehampton's proximity to France and the existence of the Railway Wharf made it important during the First World War as an ammunition supply port for the Western Front in France. Between October 1915 and November 1918, a dozen or so small steamers shuttled between Littlehampton, Le Havre and other ports with several hundred thousand tons of ammunition and other military stores.

Patients and staff at a military hospital, Groombridge House School, Littlehampton, First World War. Groombridge House School stood in Norfolk Road and was one of a number of local establishments converted to serve as military hospitals during the war. The patients are mostly dressed in the garish 'Hospital Blues', a uniform for convalescing servicemen.

May and Wareham's newsagents, Beach Road, Wednesday 29 December 1915. Some semblance of normal life continued on the home front during the First World War, as the shop window, stocked with Christmas gifts, suggests. However, there are signs of the onset of 'total war': 'compulsion' in the headlines refers to military conscription, which was introduced in 1916.

Children at the unveiling of Littlehampton War Memorial, September 1921. A total of 217 Littlehampton men were killed in the First World War - between 5 and 10 per cent of the town's adult male population. Nearly 200 families in the town lost at least one of their menfolk and there are no figures available for the numbers of servicemen who came back injured in body or mind. How many of the children in this photograph, one wonders, had lost a father or an older brother?

'Digging for Victory' at Littlehampton, 1939. Joseph Robinson is shown with his first crop of wartime potatoes. Mr Robinson served in the local Fire Service during the Second World War.

Littlehampton Home Guard in a 'War Weapons Week' parade, Beach Road, June 1941. This was one of many fundraising events held in the town during the war. Despite their modern 'Dad's Army' image, the Home Guard had a very serious purpose. Those on the South Coast would have been the first to go into action if the threatened German invasion had ever materialized. Note the plywood anti-blast screens on the shop fronts.

'B' Troop, one of the troops of 30 Assault Unit (30 AU), Royal Marines, Littlehampton, May 1944. Based at Littlehampton from January 1944 until January 1945, 30 AU was an intelligence commando, used to capture secret enemy equipment and plans. Their work was demanding and dangerous and within a month of this photograph being taken 30 AU was in action in Normandy. Nearly half of the men in this photograph became casualties, with fourteen wounded and three killed.

A *Staghound* armoured car of 30 Assault Unit, near Western Road, 1944/45. 30 AU had its headquarters at 49 South Terrace but the men were billeted with local families. The Marines were popular in Littlehampton and a considerable bond grew up between them and many townspeople.

Hillyard's workforce, Second World War. David Hillyard set up his boat building business during the First World War. It became famous for building yachts but during the Second World War had to turn to the construction of small craft for the Forces. The workforce was expanded and included women workers for the first time.

MTB634, built by Osborne's of Littlehampton, during the Second World War. This vessel was one of sixteen Fairmile motor torpedo boats constructed by Osborne's during the war. The company also built naval motor launches and a wide range of landing craft and other auxiliary vessels.

Fire Service competition between the Littlehampton and Bognor firemen, 26 December 1940. This photograph was taken by Mr O.J. Cole, who was Chief Officer of Littlehampton's Fire Brigade for more than ten years from 1939. The town's fire service grew rapidly during the war, from a single station with two appliances to a headquarters station and six small sub-stations, each of the latter equipped with a trailer pump like the one shown in the photograph.

British Red Cross, Littlehampton Detachment Sussex 522, 1943. The Red Cross nurses are as follows. Back row, left to right: Sue Townsend, Gwen Rye, Iris Jackson, Joy Hamlet, Joan Harris, Stella Symes. Middle row: Kathleen Aylmore, Rosalind Lockwood, Mrs Taylor, June Marshall, Norma Proudfoot. Front row: Yvonne Fox, Violette Shoppee, Josie Stemp. Joan Harris was killed by enemy action in 1944.

Pier Road, 18 July 1942. This devastation was caused by a single bomb, dropped at about 6.20 a.m. on a Saturday. Eight people were killed, including three children, and another seventeen were injured. It was the town's worst bombing incident.

VE Day celebration, Sandfield Avenue, Wick, May 1945. Littlehampton's Second World War dead were less than half those of the First World War - 92 killed as opposed to 217 - but this did not make the grief any less and twenty of the dead were killed in air attacks on the town. The people who lived in the town through the war suffered twenty-four air raids and over 1,000 air-raid alerts - only a couple of hundred less than London. In 1945, as with the rest of the country, they still had eight years of post-war rationing ahead.

A brushwood swastika ablaze at VE Day celebrations, Sandfield Avenue, Wick, May 1945. At the end of the Second World War, organizations like ARP were quickly wound up. Within a few years, the growing Cold War between the West and the Soviet Union had led to the revival of Civil Defence and even - for a few years - the reappearance of the Home Guard.

Acknowledgements

We would like to thank Samantha Hill and Stephanie Smith at Littlehampton Museum and Debbie Friesen and the staff of Print Plus, Arun District Council, for their help with this book.

All of the photographs in this book have come from the Littlehampton Museum Collection. We would like to thank the following people who over the years have donated some of the photographic images used in this book:

Mr Adams, Mr J. Allen, Mr D. Attle, Mrs Barker, Mr W.G. Billing, Mr P. Cheney, Mr Collings, Mr E. Cooper, Mrs P. Cowles, Mr A. Cox, Mrs I. Doble, Mrs Drew, Mrs V. Dyer, the late Alfred Farmer, Mrs B. Greenshields, Mr Hewitt, Holmes Campbell Solicitors, Mr Humphrey, Mr H. Jackson, Mr Jones, Mrs Keith, Miss P. King, Miss J. Last, Mrs Y. Lewis, Mr F. Licence, Littlehampton Natural Science and Archaeology Society, Littlehampton Sportsfield Association, Mr P.B. Mitchell, Mrs D. Monnery, Mrs Morley, Mrs Reed, Mrs B. Robinson, the late Sidney Robinson, Rosemead Educational Trust, Mr Simmons, Mr L. Speller, Mrs Smart, the late Miss D. Stanford, Mr Stapleton, Mr and Mrs Tubb, Mrs Tutt.

We would also like to thank the following people for kindly granting their permission for the reproduction of copyright photographs in this book: Mr J.R.B. Arthur, Mrs Calcutt, Mr H. Clark, Mr Cole, Mr Cooper, Mr D.B. Clayton, DANDO Drilling International (Mr M. Fitch-Roy), Mrs Eason, Hares Group (Mr R. Newman), Mrs J. Haynes, Mrs Jean Orton, William Osborne Ltd (Mr R. Boyce), Miss A. Robinson, Mrs R.J. Ryan for photographs taken by Terry Ryan, Miss B. Stiff, the late Mr C. Stiff, Mr Philip Wells, the late Geoffrey Wells.

We apologize if, despite our best efforts, a copyright photograph has been used inadvertently or a donor has not been acknowledged.